Keep 'em Reading
BULLETIN BOARDS.

Year-round Designs for the Library and Classroom

Illustrated by Ben DeSoto

Alleyside Press®

Fort Atkinson, Wisconsin

Published by **Alleyside Press**, an imprint of Highsmith Press
Highsmith Press
W5527 Highway 106
P.O. Box 800
Fort Atkinson, Wisconsin 53538-0800
1-800-558-2110

The paper used in this publication meets the minimum requirements of American
National Standard for Information Science — Permanence of Paper for Printed
Library Material. ANSI/NISO Z39.48-1992.

Contents

Introduction

While classroom and thematic bulletin board books abound, those created especially for the library media center are few. That's why we've created a book of reading promotional bulletin boards for everyday use and special occasions alike. Each bulletin board features characters reading or holding books.

Divided into three main sections, the book groups seasonal, holiday and special event and all-occasion boards for easy reference.

Each bulletin board theme includes:

- a choice of reading and book-related slogans
- an illustration of a suggested design
- large and small bold, clean-lined patterns for easy copying and tracing
- decoration and display suggestions
- additional thematic ideas.

Creating Your Bulletin Boards

Each bulletin board pattern includes individual pieces to allow you to mix and match to meet your design and decoration needs. We have suggested one way of putting the pieces together, but we encourage you to explore other options.

The most popular, common configuration is a large, main thematic piece, surrounded by smaller pieces featuring the names of each student who has completed the reading list or some other goal. (See Fig. 1.) This simple design saves you time and makes your board easy to read and understand.

Fig. 1

To enlarge the patterns for tracing, use an opaque or overhead projector and transparency copies of the patterns. Trace onto large sheets or rolls of paper. Helpful hint: Stack and cut out like pieces to save time—and your hand!

We hope you'll find the patterns, slogans and decoration suggestions are just a springboard for your own creative ideas and displays.

Preserving Your Bulletin Boards

Use your bulletin board pieces again and again, year after year! You can laminate the individual pieces for maximum versatility, or you can laminate whole bulletin boards together. Storage is just as important as laminating. Store your pieces flat in drawers or shelves. Label the storage with the name or theme of the bulletin board for easy location by you or other staff and volunteers.

If you choose to disassemble your board, but want to recreate it at another time, taking a photo of the completed board will allow you to put it back together quickly and accurately.

Getting Kids Involved

Children love projects, and they love to be helpers. Give them the opportunity to do both by having them help assemble your bulletin boards. This could include the tracing of the patterns, creating backgrounds, cutting out pieces or making their own pieces for display. Many of the suggested decoration and display ideas include activities that get children thinking about important historic or cultural issues, ask them to explore their own thoughts and feelings or just allow them to have fun.

Special Touches

In addition to the uniqueness children's creations will lend your bulletin boards, you may also consider the following enhancements:

- use fabric, specialty papers, corrugated paper and other materials to make interesting backgrounds and borders.

- treat papers and fabrics to create unique looks, including crinkling, folding, dying and weaving.
- create three-dimensional bulletin board pieces by gluing or sewing pieces together and stuffing them with cotton batting or tissue.
- use craft materials to create special effects: glitter and glitter glue, raffia, ribbon, coated wires, etc.
- create borders to cover up uneven background edges
- don't forget paint as a substitute for drawing, or to create a special texture or look.

Table Displays

Place a table in front of your bulletin board for an easy way to tie in related books and other materials to the theme on the board. Collect related items from the school and/or community to enrich the display.

Supply Sources

Party supply stores are great sources of decorations of all kinds, and paper outlet stores offer color and size choices your standard supplier might not. If you community has a textile, rubber, plastics or other materials manufacturing plant nearby, the scraps and seconds can make great crafting materials as well.

Design Suggestion

Alternative Theme(s)

Harvest

Alternative Slogans

The following slogans are suggestions that can be used with the various art pieces supplied.

1. Harvest a Good Book!
2. Scare Up a Good Book!
3. Birds of a Feather Read Together
4. Fall For Books

Decoration and Display Suggestions

1. Set up a table display with a cornucopia spilling over with fall vegetables, corn husk dolls and related books.

2. Suspend Indian corn cobs and straw hats from the ceiling or attach to the board.

3. Write students' names and books read on paper leaves and have them "fall" from a paper tree.

4. Have the students make paper patches and write their names and books written. Post on the board. Create a border with cloth patches.

5. When using the "Harvest..." slogan, decorate the board with photos of farms. Create a border using straw from a craft store.

Design Suggestion

Alternative Theme(s)

Holidays

Alternative Slogans

The following slogans are suggestions that can be used with the various art pieces supplied.

1. Warm Up with a Good Book!

2. Chill Out and Read!

3. Scarf Up a Good Book!

4. Reading Makes the Winter Bearable

Decoration and Display Suggestions

1. Use cotton batting for snow, clear cellophane for ice and styrofoam balls for snowballs.

2. Styrofoam snowballs could be labeled with students' names and books read using a permanent marker. Hang from ceiling nearby.

3. Have students cut out snowflakes then write their names and books read for posting on the board. Hang paper icicles around area.

4. Host a mitten/scarf donation program for underprivileged children. Have students bring their donations in for use as decorations first. Good for use with "Scarf" slogan.

5. Create a fire for the bear to warm near, using yellow and red cellophane.

Design Suggestion

Alternative Theme(s)

Gardening

Alternative Slogans

The following slogans are suggestions that can be used with the various art pieces supplied.

1. Bloom with Books!
2. Cultivate Your Mind — Read!
3. Plant Yourself in a Good Book
4. Take Root in Books

Decoration and Display Suggestions

1. Use seed packs or a garden hose for a border.
2. Set up a table display with toy gardening tools and books in a wheelbarrow or fill terra cotta pots with fake flowers and books.
3. Make the flower grow taller as students read more books.
4. Using the "Plant Yourself..." slogan, put each student's picture in the center of the smaller flower illustration and display on the board.
5. Show what is seen both above ground as well as below ground (roots, worms, etc.). Good for use with "Take Root..." slogan.
6. Have students create new book titles relating to plants. Display them on the board.

Design Suggestion

Alternative Theme(s)

Vacation

Back to School

Alternative Slogans

The following slogans are suggestions that can be used with the various art pieces supplied.

1. What I Did on My Summer Vacation

2. Spend Your Summer Reading

3. Travel Through the Pages of a Good Book

4. Be a Backseat Reader

Decoration and Display Suggestions

1. Drape brightly colored beach towels around the edges of the bulletin board.

2. Use sandpaper to create a beach, and rippled blue cellophane or plastic wrap for water.

3. Create a table display in front with children's flotation devices and pail and shovel sets filled with books about summer activities.

4. When featuring the car illustration and the slogan, "Travel Through the Pages..." or "Be a Backseat..." create a border with old license plates or travel maps.

5. Before summer or in fall: display students' vacation destinations or activities. Good for use with "What I Did..." slogan.

READ BOOKS

READ A LOT

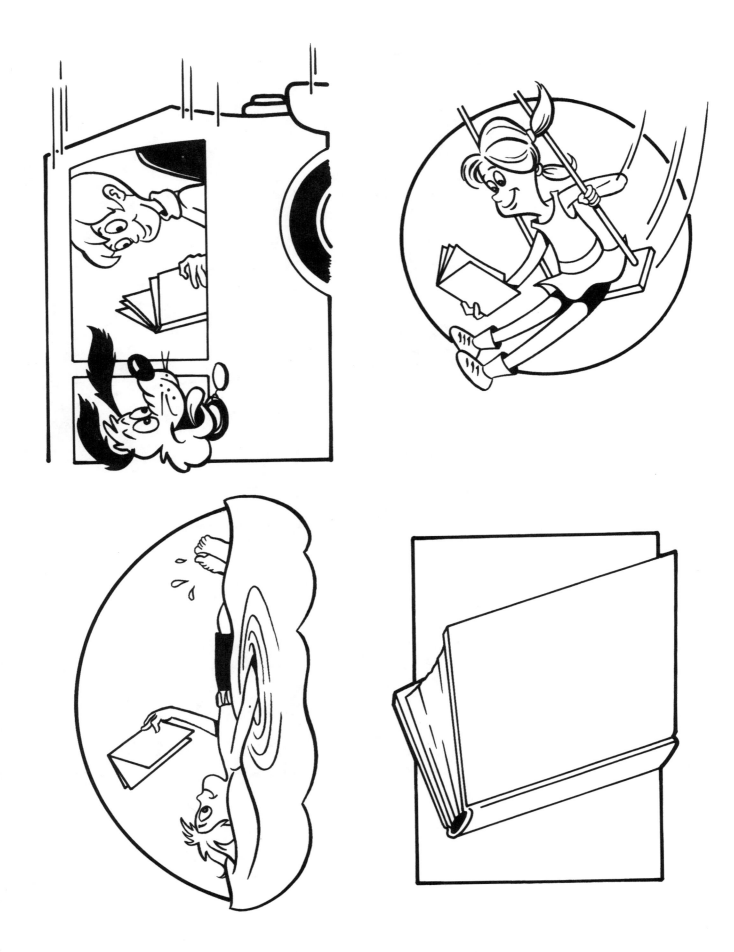

Design Suggestion

Alternative Theme(s)

Friendship

Alternative Slogans

The following slogans are suggestions that can be used with the various art pieces supplied.

1. Welcome Back!

2. Make Friends with Books — Read!

3. Books Rule the School

4. Books are in a Class by Themselves

Decoration and Display Suggestions

1. Create a border using rulers (craft stores carry multi-packs) or large crayons made with colored craft paper.

2. Set up a table display with a backpack overflowing with school supplies and books.

3. Post school-aged photos of faculty, and have students match names to faces. Or, match current faculty photos with their favorite books.

4. Have students make up new school subjects and textbook titles. Post results.

5. Using the "Make Friends..." slogan, set up a table display of books on friendship.

6. Using the "Make Friends..." slogan, start a book club for students to discuss books.

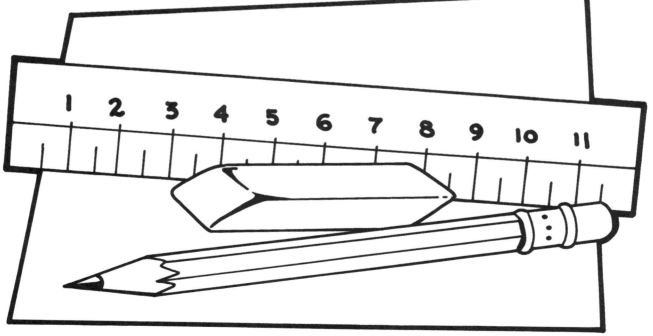

Design Suggestion

Alternative Theme(s)

Scary Stories

Alternative Slogans

The following slogans are suggestions that can be used with the various art pieces supplied.

1. Trick or Treat — Books are Neat!
2. I Like Booooks!
3. Books are Spooktacular!
4. Books are a Real Treat!

Decoration and Display Suggestions

1. Drape white sheets along the edge of the bulletin board to create ghost-like images.
2. Locate a skeleton model to hang in the area.
3. Have each student make a pumpkin face and write a favorite book on it. Display.
4. Set up a table display with a trick-or-treat bag spilling over with candy wrappers and scary stories.
5. Use black paper for the background and create a border with plastic spiders or candy wrappers.
6. As students finish reading books, write each title on a paper candy corn design and post.

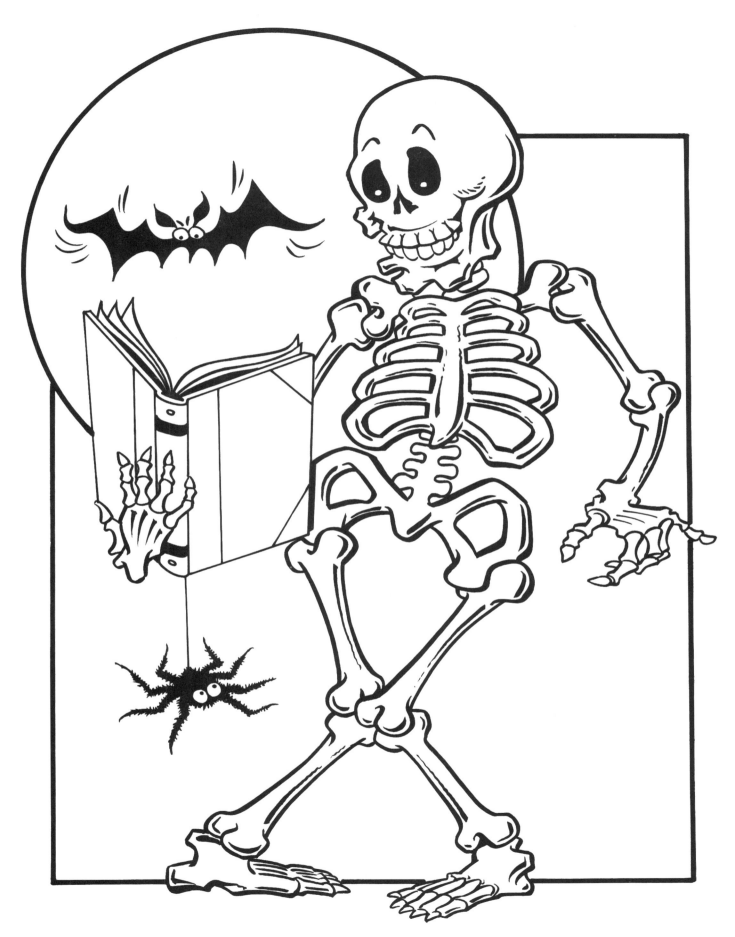

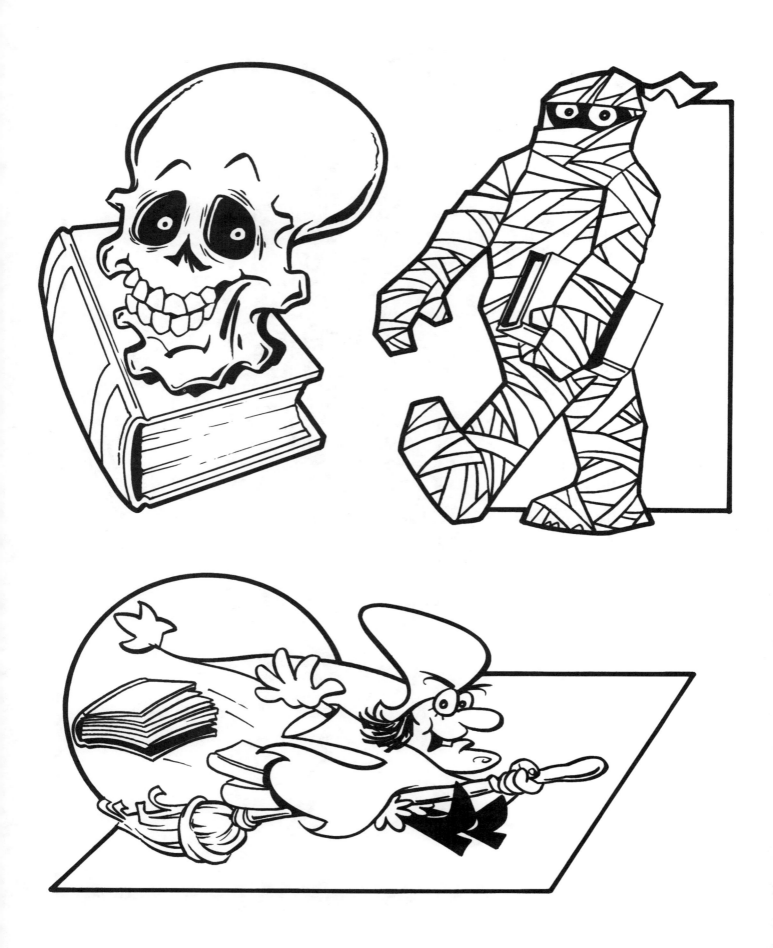

Design Suggestion

Alternative Theme(s)

Fall

Harvest

Alternative Slogans

The following slogans are suggestions that can be used with the various art pieces supplied.

1. Gobble up a Good Book!

2. Books are a Feast for the Mind

3. Give Thanks for Books

4. Harvest a Good Book

Decoration and Display Suggestions

1. Write book titles on the turkey's feathers.

2. Set up a table display with all of the foods people eat for Thanksgiving, complete with place setting. Place a book on the plate. The food can be plastic models or paper cut-outs.

3. Use brown and dark orange paper for the background and leaves or feathers for the border. Feathers can be bought at craft stores.

4. Have students collect real leaves to display. Help them identify the trees they came from, then label and attach to the board.

5. Using the "Give Thanks..." slogan, have students answer: "For what are you thankful?" Post responses on bulletin board.

Design Suggestion

Alternative Theme(s)

Book Lovers

Love Your Library

Alternative Slogans

The following slogans are suggestions that can be used with the various art pieces supplied.

1. LOVE My Library
2. We Love Reading!
3. Put Your Heart Into a Good Book!
4. Books Are My Valentine!

Decoration and Display Suggestions

1. Make the background with red, white, pink or all three colors of paper. Create a border using lace or paper doilies.

2. Have students write Valentines to their favorite authors. Post on the bulletin board.

3. Using the "Books Are My..." slogan, have students write their favorite titles on paper hearts and post on the board.

4. Set up a table display featuring the many different kinds of love, including photos and related books.

5. Have students come up with new candy heart slogans relating to books and reading. Post them on hearts on the board.

Design Suggestion

Alternative Theme(s)

America

Fourth of July

Alternative Slogans

The following slogans are suggestions that can be used with the various art pieces supplied.

1. Reading Rocks!

2. Books are Monumental!

3. Read with Pride

4. America Reads

Decoration and Display Suggestions

1. Ask students what author they would nominate for a place on Mount Read-more. Post the responses along with book titles and perhaps the authors' photos on the board.

2. Set up a table display with patriotic items and books on the U.S. presidency. Have students vote for their favorite book.

3. Make a background using brown or gray paper for the ground and blue for the sky, with a border of stars and stripes.

4. Using the "Reading Rocks" slogan, cut/paint styrofoam to make rocks and attach to board.

5. Have students "travel" to Mount Read-more as they complete a reading list.

I-rish I Had More Time to READ

Design Suggestion

Alternative Theme(s)

Ireland

March

Alternative Slogans

The following slogans are suggestions that can be used with the various art pieces supplied.

1. Books are a Pot of Gold!
2. Leapin' Leprechauns — Read!
3. March Into a Good Book
4. Books are Charming

Decoration and Display Suggestions

1. Using the "Books are a..." slogan, set up a table display with a large, black, cast iron pot spilling over with plastic or gold foil chocolate coins and books about St. Patrick and/or Ireland.

2. Ask, "What's at the end of your rainbow?" Have students reply on shamrocks and post.

3. Make a bright yellow background with a shamrock and mushroom border.

4. Have students draw and color rainbows, then add their favorite book titles to each stripe in the rainbow. Post on the board.

5. Advance students along a large rainbow as they complete a reading list.

Celebrate National Library Week!

Design Suggestion

Alternative Theme(s)

Fourth of July

Alternative Slogans

The following slogans are suggestions that can be used with the various art pieces supplied.

1. Celebrate with Books!

2. Reading is a Blast!

3. Launch Your Imagination — Read!

4. Stars, Stripes and Books Forever!

Decoration and Display Suggestions

1. Have students cut out paper stars and write their name and book read for posting.

2. Use cotton batting for clouds and red, white and blue crepe paper streamers for borders.

3. Set up a table display with a picnic basket overflowing with plates, cups and related books. Use a picnic blanket as a "table cloth."

4. When using the "Stars and Stripes..." slogan, have students fill each line of a flag with a book title they've read.

5. Using one parachute and books illustration per student, write their name on the parachute and the books they've read on each book.

National Library Week Theme *Keep 'em Reading Bulletin Boards* **45**

Design Suggestion

Alternative Theme(s)

Winning

Alternative Slogans

The following slogans are suggestions that can be used with the various art pieces supplied.

1. Tackle a Good Book!

2. Make a Play for Books!

3. Reading: A Sport for all Seasons

4. Get in the Game — Read!

Decoration and Display Suggestions

1. Create a football or soccer field using green paper and white paint. Use pennants as a border. Make the soccer and footballs three-dimensional and hang nearby. Advance the ball down the field for each book read.

2. Have students cut out athlete photos from magazines and attach their photo to the athlete's body. Display with their favorite books.

3. Have students make up a game, including the rules, players, equipment and mascot.

4. Set up a table display using athletic equipment, trophies and related books.

5. Have students write their favorite books on paper pennants and display on the board.

Dinosaurs

Design Suggestion

Alternative Theme(s)

Time Periods

Alternative Slogans

The following slogans are suggestions that can be used with the various art pieces supplied.

1. Roar Into Reading

2. Stomp Into a Good Book

3. Since Time Began, Books Ruled the Land

4. Make Tracks — Read!

Decoration and Display Suggestions

1. Using the "Make Tracks..." slogan, have students create real or imaginary footprints for display, including the name of the dinosaur that made it.

2. Create a volcano in the background using brown craft paper with read and yellow cellophane for lava.

3. Give the board a tropical look using shredded green paper for tall grass.

4. Using the "Since Time Began..." slogan, have students recreate the Earth's time line in major periods.

5. Set up a table display with dinosaur models and books.

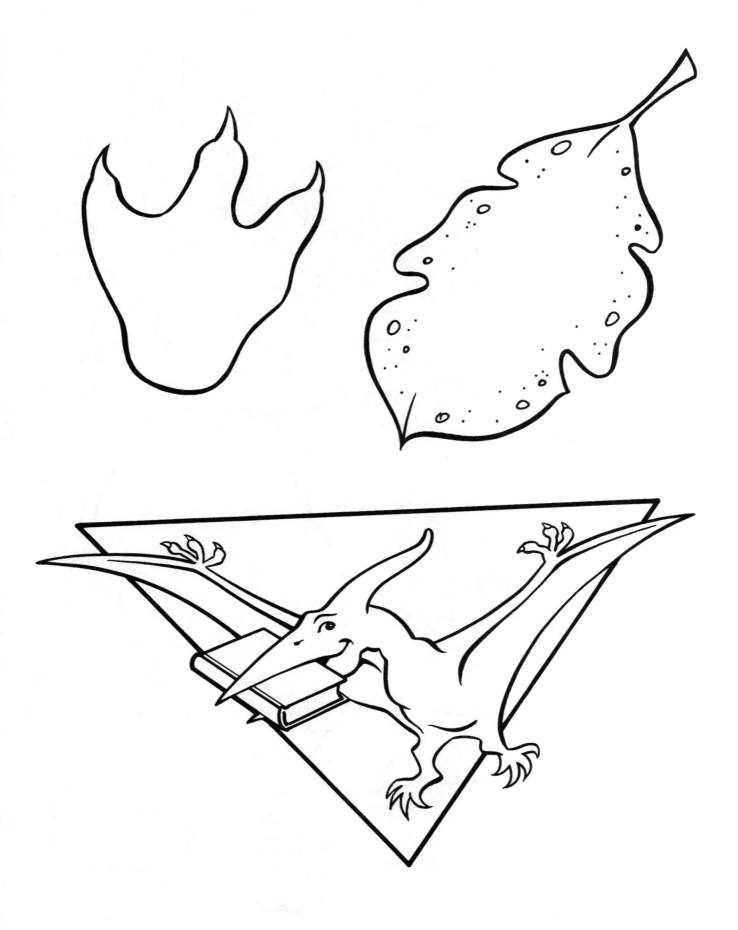

Design Suggestion

Alternative Theme(s)

Fantasy

Alternative Slogans

The following slogans are suggestions that can be used with the various art pieces supplied.

1. Cast a Spell — Read!

2. Conjure Up a Good Book!

3. Make Magic with Books!

4. Enter a Magical World with Books

Decoration and Display Suggestions

1. Drape metallic fabric around edges of the bulletin board to look like a cape.

2. Using the slogan, "Enter a Magical World…," have students describe in writing an imaginary land, including the landscape, the people, creatures, sounds, smells, etc. for posting.

3. Create spider webs using string or yarn and drape across the board or around the area.

4. Set up a table display with a large, old book from which magical things appear; they could either be drawn by students for posting above, or objects you place on the table nearby.

5. Use black paper sprinkled with glitter as a background.

53

Design Suggestion

Alternative Theme(s)

Rodeos

Alternative Slogans

The following slogans are suggestions that can be used with the various art pieces supplied.

1. Lasso a Good Book!

2. Get a Kick out of Reading

3. Hats Off to Books

4. Join the Reading Rodeo!

Decoration and Display Suggestions

1. Make cacti using green foam core board with toothpicks as spines. Use sandpaper for the ground and grapevine for tumbleweeds. Drape a southwestern-style blanket along the edge of the bulletin board.

2. Set up a table display with cowboy boots, hats, lassos, horseshoes and related books.

3. Write each student's name and favorite book on the cowboy hats and place them on their school pictures.

4. Move the "Book-a-roo" illustration along the western trail for every book or ten books read.

5. Using the "Join the..." slogan, have students draw or describe a day at the rodeo. Display.

READ

Design Suggestion

Alternative Theme(s)

Adventure

Treasure Hunting

Alternative Slogans

The following slogans are suggestions that can be used with the various art pieces supplied.

1. Books are a Treasure
2. Unlock the Treasure of Reading
3. Treasure Your Library
4. At Storytime, the Water's Fine!

Decoration and Display Suggestions

1. Copy a set of bubbles for each student, and add book titles to it as they read.

2. Use blue and green cellophane for water and sandpaper for the ocean floor. Hang plastic fish in area.

3. Attach sea shells and starfish to the board or display on a table in front with related books.

4. Set up a table display with swim goggles, snorkeling masks, flippers and related books.

5. Using any of the "Treasure..." slogans, set up a table display with a steamer trunk full of plastic or gold foil chocolate coins, skeleton keys and strings of fake pearls. Attach craft store plastic gems that are flat on one side.

Design Suggestion

Alternative Theme(s)

Nature Conservation

Alternative Slogans

The following slogans are suggestions that can be used with the various art pieces supplied.

1. Swing Into a Good Book
2. Leapin' Lizards — Read!
3. Hang Out with a Great Tale!
4. Go Bananas — Read!

Decoration and Display Suggestions

1. Hang plastic fruit and vines around area.
2. Place half the trunk on the left side of the bulletin board, with leafy branches stretching across the board. Designate one leaf per student with their names and the titles of the books they've read.
3. Create a bamboo and leaf border.
4. Set up a table display of the diversity of plant, animal and insect life in the rain forest, including plastic and plush models and related books.
5. Assign students to teams named leopard, gorilla, snake, parrot, etc. and have each team read about their animal and report to group.

Design Suggestion

Alternative Theme(s)

Ocean Life

Alternative Slogans

The following slogans are suggestions that can be used with the various art pieces supplied.

1. So Many Books, So Little Tentacles
2. The More You Read, The More You Know
3. Books are a Tidal Wave of Fun
4. Submerse Yourself in a Good Book

Decoration and Display Suggestions

1. Create a seaweed background, using blue, green and teal paper cut in wavy strips and a sea floor made with sandpaper. Create a watery background using blue and green cellophane or plastic wrap.

2. Copy one octopus per student, and have the students write the titles they've read on each book.

3. Have students imagine a sea creature and draw it or describe it in writing for posting.

4. Make the octopus' suction cups realistic using real suction cups glued to its tentacles.

5. Hang plastic fish and seaweed in the area.

Additional Book Patterns